LET'S TALK ABOUT
BEING
CARELESS

By Joy Berry
Illustrated by John Costanza

CHILDRENS PRESS®
CHICAGO

Let's talk about BEING CARELESS.

You are BEING CARELESS when
you act as though
you do not care about yourself.

You are BEING CARELESS when
you act as though
you do not care about
the people and things around you.

Being careless
can cause you to hurt yourself.

Being careless
can cause you to hurt other people.

Being careless
can cause you to damage or destroy something.

11

It is not good to be careless.

You need to BE CAREFUL instead.

When you are careful you act
as though you care about yourself.

When you are careful you act
as though you care about the
people and things around you.

13

Be careful.
   OBEY THE RULES.

The adults who are responsible for you know what you need to do to keep yourself and others safe.

They also know what you need to do to take care of the things around you.

The rules they make can
help you be careful.

Be careful.
    PAY ATTENTION.

Think about what you are doing.
If you do, you will make fewer mistakes.

Be careful.
SLOW DOWN.

If you do, you will avoid accidents
that often happen when you are in a hurry.

Be careful.
   LOOK WHERE YOU ARE GOING.

If you do, you will avoid
tripping and bumping into things.

Be careful.
 LISTEN TO THE PEOPLE AND
 SOUNDS AROUND YOU.

They may be warning you that danger is near.

If you listen and respond to them,
you may avoid a dangerous situation.

Be careful.
   DO NOT PLAY TOO ROUGHLY.

Someone might get hurt, or
something might get broken
if you play too roughly.

No one will get hurt, and
nothing will get broken if
you play carefully.

Be careful.
DO NOT PLAY WITH DANGEROUS THINGS.

If you avoid playing with dangerous
things, you will avoid hurting
yourself and others.

Be careful.
DO NOT PLAY IN DANGEROUS PLACES.

If you avoid playing in dangerous places,
you will avoid hurting yourself and others.

29

It is not good to be careless.
It is better for you to be careful.

About the Author
Joy Berry is the author of more than 150 self-help books for children. She has advanced degrees and credentials in both education and human development and specializes in working with children from birth to twelve years of age. Joy is the founder of the Institute of Living Skills. She is the mother of a son, Christopher, and a daughter, Lisa.